I0813579

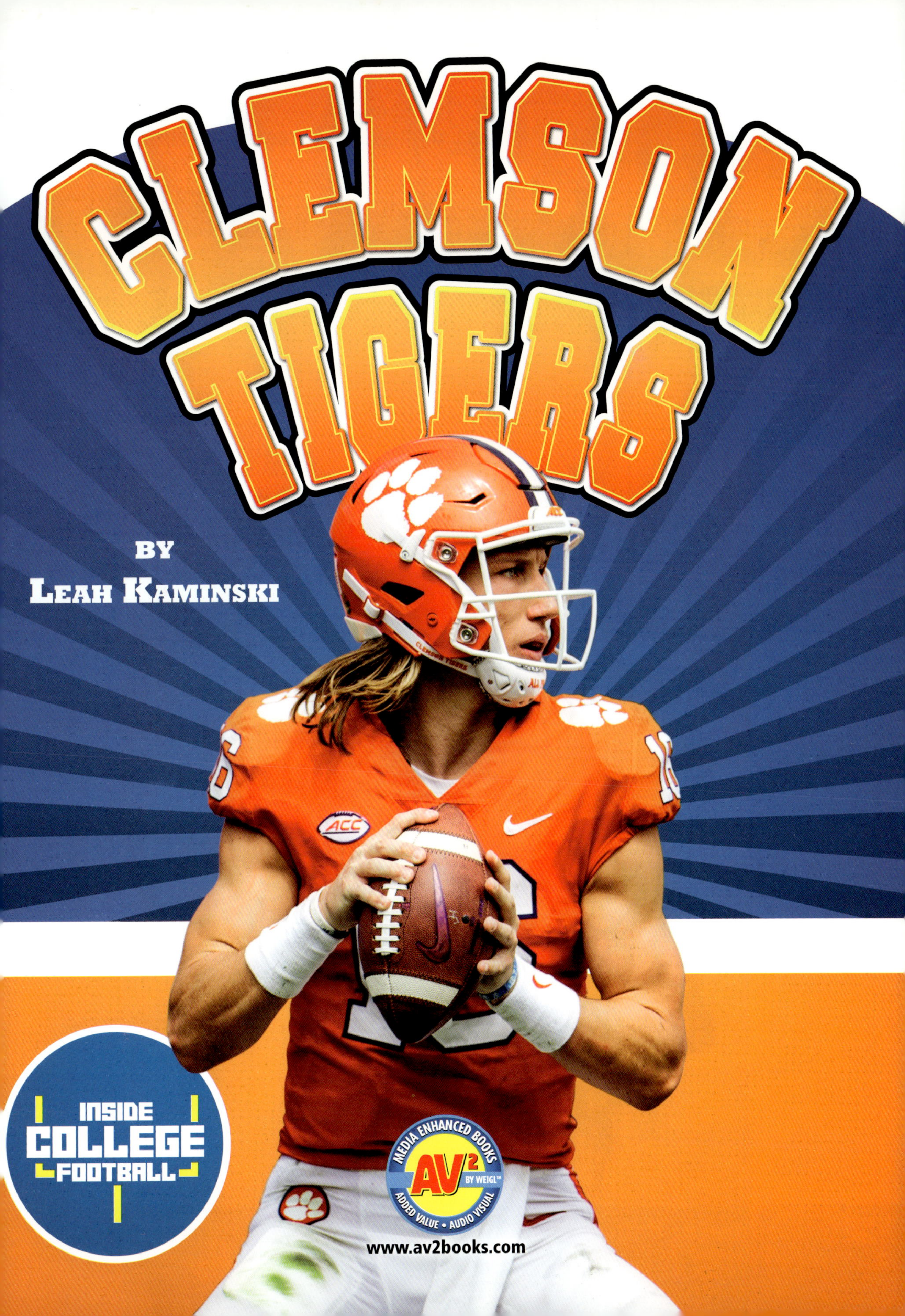
CLEMSON TIGERS
BY
LEAH KAMINSKI
INSIDE
COLLEGE
FOOTBALL
MEDIA ENHANCED BOOKS
AV2
BY WEIGL
ADDED VALUE • AUDIO VISUAL
www.av2books.com

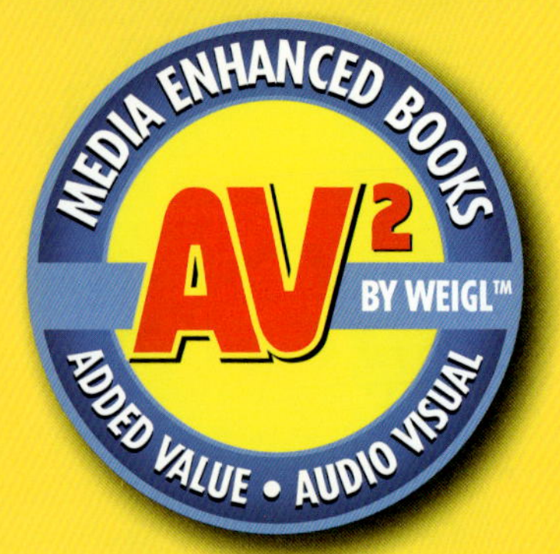

Go to **www.av2books.com**, and enter this book's unique code.

BOOK CODE

AVV94928

AV² by Weigl brings you media enhanced books that support active learning.

AV² provides enriched content that supplements and complements this book. Weigl's AV² books strive to create inspired learning and engage young minds in a total learning experience.

Your AV² Media Enhanced books come alive with...

Audio
Listen to sections of the book read aloud.

Key Words
Study vocabulary, and complete a matching word activity.

Video
Watch informative video clips.

Quizzes
Test your knowledge.

Embedded Weblinks
Gain additional information for research.

Slideshow
View images and captions, and prepare a presentation.

Try This!
Complete activities and hands-on experiments.

... and much, much more!

Published by AV² by Weigl
350 5th Avenue, 59th Floor
New York, NY 10118
Website: www.av2books.com

Library of Congress Control Number: 2018968196

ISBN 978-1-7911-0062-9 (hardcover)
ISBN 978-1-7911-0063-6 (multi-user eBook)
ISBN 978-1-7911-0064-3 (single-user eBook)

Printed in Guangzhou, China
1 2 3 4 5 6 7 8 9 0 23 22 21 20 19

042019
102318

Project Coordinator: Jared Siemens Designer: Terry Paulhus

The publisher acknowledges Alamy, Getty Images, and Wikimedia Commons as its primary image suppliers for this title.

Clemson Tigers

CONTENTS

Introduction

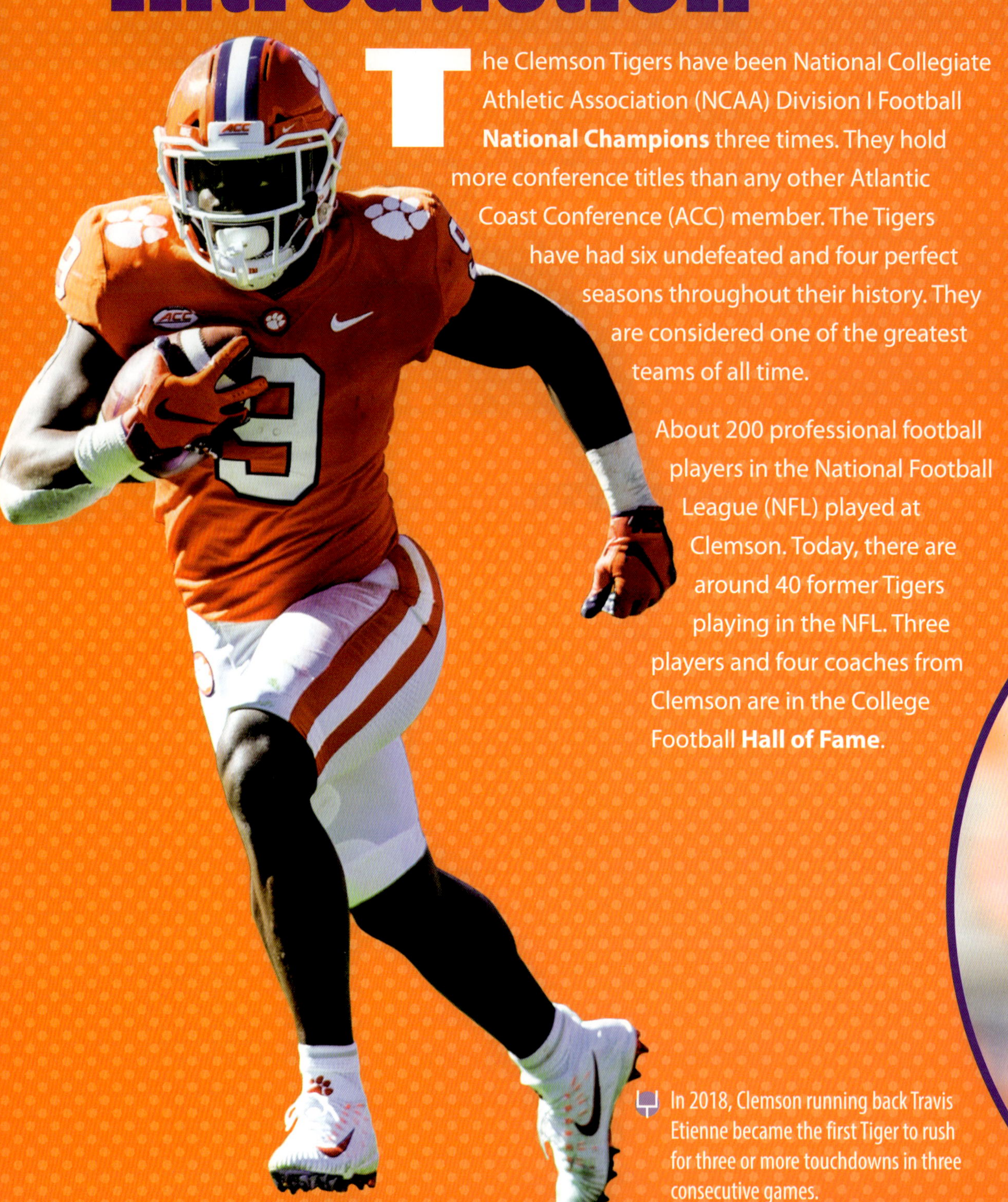

The Clemson Tigers have been National Collegiate Athletic Association (NCAA) Division I Football **National Champions** three times. They hold more conference titles than any other Atlantic Coast Conference (ACC) member. The Tigers have had six undefeated and four perfect seasons throughout their history. They are considered one of the greatest teams of all time.

About 200 professional football players in the National Football League (NFL) played at Clemson. Today, there are around 40 former Tigers playing in the NFL. Three players and four coaches from Clemson are in the College Football **Hall of Fame**.

In 2018, Clemson running back Travis Etienne became the first Tiger to rush for three or more touchdowns in three consecutive games.

Clemson is still considered a top team, winning four ACC titles in a row from 2015 to 2018. They are known for having excellent offense and defense. The Tigers also have a tradition of strong **recruiting** and coaching and should continue to be one of the top college football teams.

Wide receiver Will Brown made his Clemson debut against ACC rival University of Louisville in 2018.

CLEMSON

Stadium Frank Howard Field at Clemson Memorial Stadium ("Death Valley")

Division Atlantic Coast Conference (ACC) Atlantic

Head Coach Dabo Swinney

Location Clemson, South Carolina

National Championships 3

Nicknames The Tigers

4
ACC Titles in a Row

50
Wins by 2017 Senior Class

26
Former Tigers with Super Bowl Rings

81,500
Seats in Clemson Memorial Stadium

History

The Clemson-South Carolina game is called the **"Palmetto Bowl."**

The 1959 Sugar Bowl pitted the Tigers of Clemson against the Tigers of Louisiana State University (LSU). Clemson's defense was fierce, but LSU scored the one and only touchdown of the game.

Since their inception in 1896, the Tigers have been a successful team. They have won more than 700 games. Their team name has many origin stories, including that their long hair and striped uniforms made them look like tigers. The most accepted story is that they wanted to honor Walter Riggs, their first coach. Riggs came from Auburn University, whose team is also the Tigers.

Clemson University was a founding member of the ACC in 1953. Clemson and the University of South Carolina have been rivals since the second game of their first season. The rivalry is one of the oldest college rivalries and spans both athletics and academics. Since 1960, the two teams have played every year in late November.

The Tigers have many long-running game-day rituals. Homecoming has been a tradition since 1914. "Tigerama" began in 1957 and is one of the country's largest student-run pep rallies. Tigerama kicks off homecoming weekend. Since 1974, the First Friday Parade has been held the Friday afternoon before the first home football game to celebrate the new football season.

The Tigers' first head coach, Walter Riggs, went on to become president of Clemson University in 1911 and led the school for 14 years.

The Stadium

Before their home stadium in Charlotte, North Carolina, was completed in 1996, the NFL's Carolina Panthers played home games at Clemson's Memorial Stadium.

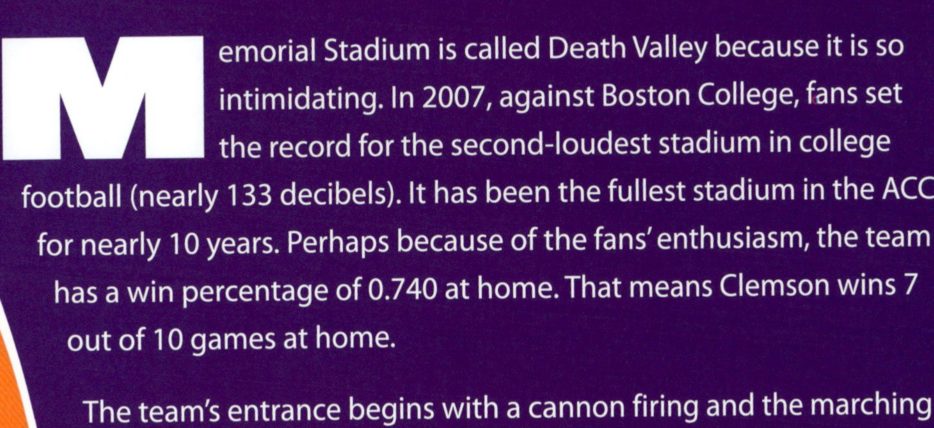

Memorial Stadium is called Death Valley because it is so intimidating. In 2007, against Boston College, fans set the record for the second-loudest stadium in college football (nearly 133 decibels). It has been the fullest stadium in the ACC for nearly 10 years. Perhaps because of the fans' enthusiasm, the team has a win percentage of 0.740 at home. That means Clemson wins 7 out of 10 games at home.

The team's entrance begins with a cannon firing and the marching band playing "Tiger Rag." Since 1942, the team has run down the hill next to the field. Since 1966, they have rubbed Howard's Rock on the way. The rock is from Death Valley, California, and was a gift to Coach Frank Howard.

Two Clemson football players helped design the first stadium. The first version of the stadium had 20,000 seats, and it was built for $125,000. Upper decks were added in 1978 and 1983 for a total of 78,000 seats. In 2006, the stadium was expanded to its current capacity of 81,500.

The Clemson Tigers have been running down "the Hill" before almost every game since 1942. The team's charge into Death Valley is rated one of the best entrances in college football.

Where They Play

Welcome to Memorial Stadium, nicknamed Death Valley. Opponents fear it and Clemson students and players love it. The players emerge, surrounded by the roar of fans. The bleachers are filled with orange and white. The Tigers are ready to play.

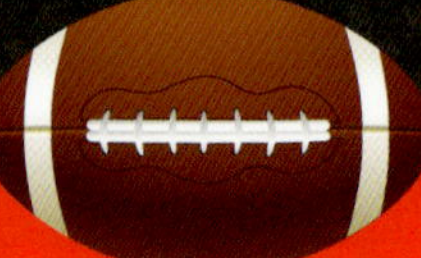

ACC ATLANTIC

1. **Boston College**
   Chestnut Hill, Massachusetts
2. ☆ **Clemson University**
   Clemson, South Carolina
3. **Florida State University**
   Tallahassee, Florida
4. **North Carolina State University**
   Raleigh, North Carolina
5. **Syracuse University**
   Syracuse, New York
6. **University of Louisville**
   Louisville, Kentucky
7. **University of Notre Dame**
   Notre Dame, Indiana
8. **Wake Forest University**
   Winston-Salem, North Carolina

Arena
Clemson Memorial Stadium

Location
Clemson, South Carolina

Broke Ground
1941

Completed
1942

Surface
Real Grass

Features
- The largest stadium in the ACC, and one of the largest in the United States
- Playing surface named Frank Howard Field in 1974, after the legendary coach
- Scroll of Honor in Memorial Park across from the stadium, memorializing 491 Clemson military personnel killed in the line of duty

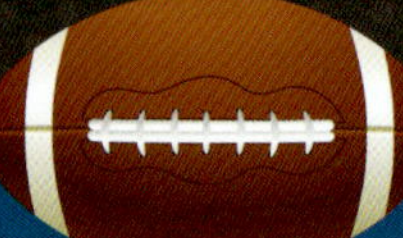

ACC COASTAL

1. **Duke University**
   Durham, North Carolina
2. **Georgia Institute of Technology**
   Atlanta, Georgia
3. **University of Miami**
   Coral Gables, Florida
4. **University of North Carolina at Chapel Hill**
   Chapel Hill, North Carolina
5. **University of Pittsburgh**
   Pittsburgh, Pennsylvania
6. **University of Virginia**
   Charlottesville, Virginia
7. **Virginia Polytechnic Institute and State University**
   Blacksburg, Virginia

NEW HAMPSHIRE
MAINE
VERMONT
1
MASSACHUSETTS
5
NEW YORK
RHODE ISLAND
CONNECTICUT
NEW JERSEY
5
PENNSYLVANIA
6
DELAWARE
MARYLAND
WASHINGTON, D.C.
NORTH DAKOTA
WISCONSIN
MINNESOTA
MICHIGAN
SOUTH DAKOTA
IOWA
OHIO
NEBRASKA
7
ILLINOIS
INDIANA
WEST VIRGINIA
VIRGINIA
7
1
KENTUCKY
4
KANSAS
MISSOURI
6
NORTH CAROLINA
8
TENNESSEE
4
SOUTH CAROLINA
2
OKLAHOMA
ARKANSAS
2
Atlantic Ocean
MISSISSIPPI
ALABAMA
GEORGIA
FLORIDA
TEXAS
LOUISIANA
3
3
Gulf of Mexico
LEGEND
Home Stadium
ACC Atlantic
ACC Coastal
United States
Other Countries
Water
SCALE
0 miles
500 miles
0 kilometers
500 km

The Uniforms

New helmets provided in 2017 have very advanced **safety features**, including a stabilization system to protect players' heads.

Wide receiver Amari Rodgers had 19 receptions for 123 yards as a substitute in 14 games during his freshman year. By his sophomore year, Rodgers had earned a starting position with the Tigers.

Clemson University's official colors are purple and burnt orange, but orange and white are the most-used Tigers uniform colors. The Tigers once wore pale purple and gold. In 1931, Coach Jess Neely chose deep purple and burnt orange because the paler colors faded too much when washed. In 1970, Clemson announced the use of its new **logo**, a tiger paw. It began appearing on helmets that year.

HOME

AWAY

The Tigers currently wear orange or white jerseys, white pants, and white shoes with orange laces. There are tiger paws on the shoulder pads and pants. Clemson's present-day helmets are simple. They are orange, with a white paw print on each side, and a purple and white stripe down the middle. The team also uses "pride stickers" on their helmets. These stickers mark individual and team accomplishments.

Defensive end Shaq Lawson earned dozens of tiger paws for his impressive tackles and sacks. His overall contribution to the team made him a valuable leader in Clemson's defensive line.

Student Athletes

Wide receiver Justyn Ross was recruited by top teams in his home state of Alabama, but he chose to play for Clemson instead.

Being a college student athlete is hard work. Student athletes have to perform well on the football field and in the classroom. Clemson student athletes are required to meet a minimum grade point average and attend all of their classes. Coach Dabo Swinney has said, "I want my players to win championships, but my number one goal is for my players to graduate." Student athletes get academic help at Vickery Hall, the first facility in the country of its kind. The Tigers were second to Stanford University in an academic ranking of the top 25 football teams in 2016.

Many student athletes are given athletic scholarships. An athletic scholarship is a financial aid agreement between the athlete and the college or university. Athletes who do not receive an athletic scholarship can also be "walk-on" members of the team. This means they are on the team, but without athletic financial aid. Clemson typically offers the maximum number of football scholarships allowed, which is 85.

Clemson invested more than $15 million into athletic student aid, including scholarships, in 2016. While some schools depend on student fees and other school funds for athletics, the Tigers do not. The university was third in athletics revenue in the ACC in 2017. It makes money from ticket sales, contributions, and rights and licensing fees.

Clemson students and other Clemson Tigers fans flock to Memorial Stadium for home games every season, thanks in part to the school's game-day traditions and Clemson's winning record.

Bowl Games

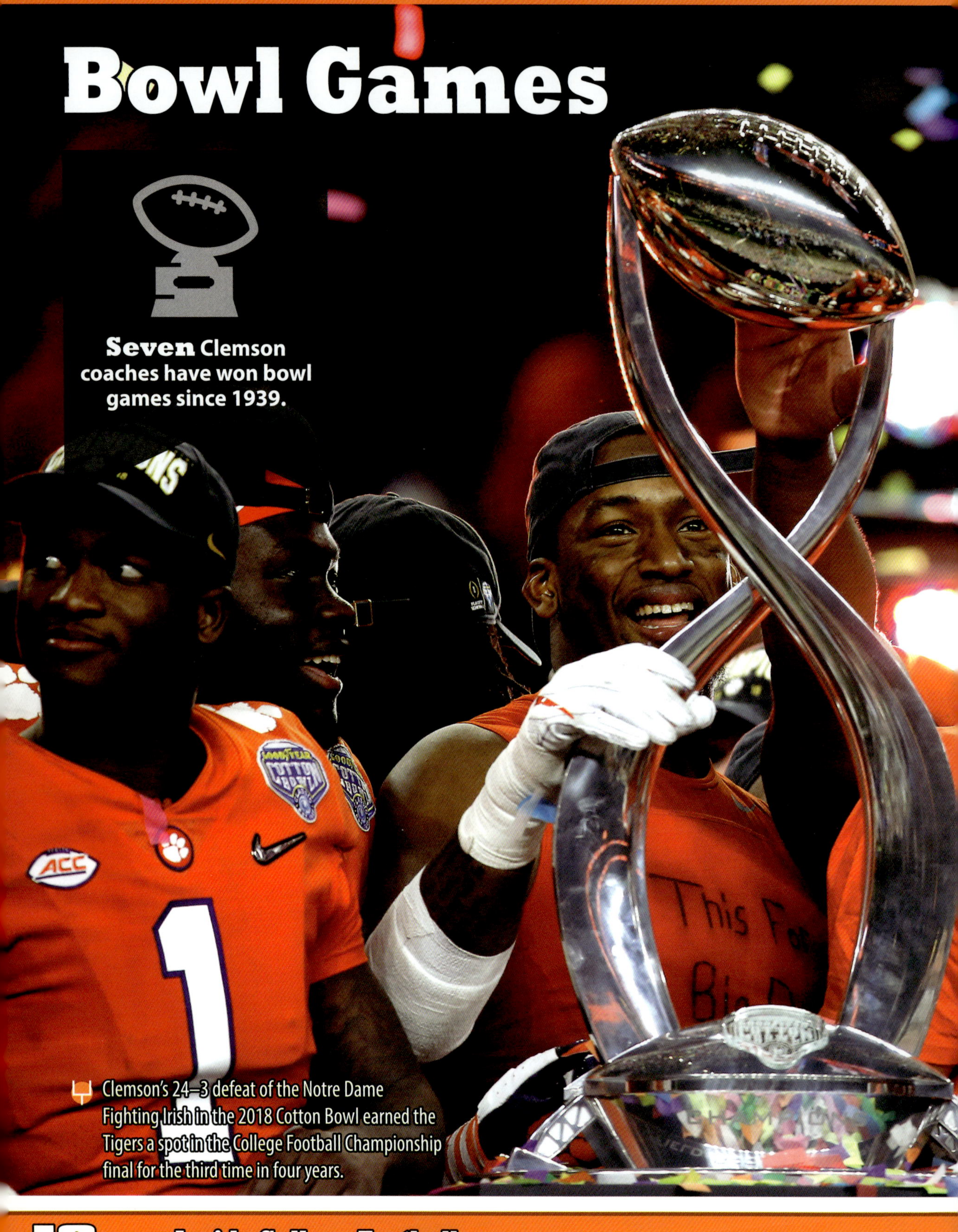

Seven Clemson coaches have won bowl games since 1939.

Clemson's 24–3 defeat of the Notre Dame Fighting Irish in the 2018 Cotton Bowl earned the Tigers a spot in the College Football Championship final for the third time in four years.

Bowl games are a unique sports tradition in college football. In the beginning of college football, there was no true **postseason**. Today, a variety of postseason bowl games are played. Bowl games give teams the opportunity to continue striving for recognition and victory after the end of regular play. There are currently 40 bowl games played in various combinations each year. These games are chosen with input from teams, sponsors, and the College Football Playoff Committee. The game matchups are announced in December.

Clemson's overall record in bowl games is 22–20. This includes a current streak of 13 appearances, and two stretches of five consecutive wins. The Tigers rank in the top 20 teams for all-time bowl appearances and wins. They won their first three bowl games ever, starting with the Cotton Bowl against Boston College in 1940. Clemson won the 1981 National Championship after a 22–15 victory over the University of Nebraska Cornhuskers in the Orange Bowl.

Clemson competed with the Alabama Crimson Tide in the Sugar Bowl at the end of the 2017 season for a chance to play for the National Championship. Alabama defeated the Tigers 26–6.

The Coaches

In 1999, Clemson coach **Tommy Bowden** faced his father, Bobby Bowden, and the Florida State Seminoles in what came to be known as the "Bowden Bowl." The game drew the largest crowd in Memorial Stadium history.

In 2018, the Tigers were named the College Football National Champions. Dabo Swinney led the Tigers to victory over the Alabama Crimson Tide 44 to 16.

The Tigers have had 25 head coaches since the team's first season. Seven coaches have taken the team to bowl games. Four have won conference championships. Coaches John Heisman, Jess Neely, Danny Ford, and Frank Howard are all College Football Hall of Fame members. Coach Ford and Coach Dabo Swinney led Clemson to their three National Championships. Howard and Ford are also members of the Clemson Ring of Honor.

JOHN HEISMAN John Heisman is a major figure in college football history. A trophy was even named after him. He coached Clemson football from 1900 to 1903. Heisman made Clemson one of the great early collegiate teams by focusing on strategy instead of strength. He was a source of many **innovations**, such as saying "hike!" at the start of a play.

FRANK HOWARD Frank Howard was not just a coach, he was also a player. He coached from 1940 to 1969. After he stopped coaching, he continued to be a part of the team until his death in 1996. When he retired, he had been head football coach at a major institution longer than anyone else in the United States. He has the most wins of any coach in Clemson history.

DABO SWINNEY Dabo Swinney has coached Clemson since 2008. He lead the Tigers to their 2016 and 2018 National Championship wins. He has the second-most wins ever for Clemson. He is also a four-time National Coach of the Year. Swinney's locker room list of goals and values ends with "Have Fun!" and he has been heard to say, "The key to coaching is love."

The Mascot

The Tiger once did a total of 465 push-ups during a high-scoring game against Wake Forest University in 1981.

The Tiger mascot dates back to 1954. It is one of the most famous mascots in the country, and one of the most athletic. The Tiger does as many push-ups as the team has points. As the Tigers continue to score, the push-ups increase. This tradition began with the 1978 mascot. The Tiger suit has huge, bright yellow eyes and bright orange fur. The Tiger's intense eyes are why it was once named by CBS Sports as one of the scariest college mascots.

Since 1993, a Tiger Cub mascot has joined the Tiger on the sidelines. It is a smaller, friendlier version of the Tiger. The Cub often hugs child fans. From 1954 to 1972, a "Country Gentleman" in purple tails, a top hat, and a cane cheered the team with the Tiger.

It is a Clemson University tradition for the student who plays the Tiger to wear the costume's paws on graduation day, revealing his or her secret identity to the world.

Legends of the Past

For many players, their time with the Clemson Tigers is the start of a promising football career. These are some of the best-known football players to play for the Tigers.

Brian Dawkins

Brian Dawkins was a starting safety during all three years he played at Clemson. Dawkins was inducted into the Clemson Athletic Hall of Fame in 2009. He played in the NFL from 1996 to 2011, mostly with the Philadelphia Eagles, before retiring in 2011. Nicknamed "Weapon X," Dawkins became one of the NFL's best safeties of all time. He was the first Tiger inducted into the Pro Football Hall of Fame. Clemson established the Brian Dawkins Lifetime Achievement Award in 2013. The award honors a former player for athletic performance, leadership, and community service. Dawkins was the first recipient.

Position: Free Safety
Seasons: 1993–1995 (Clemson Tigers), 1996–2008 (Philadelphia Eagles), 2009–2011 (Denver Broncos)
Born: October 13, 1973, Jacksonville, Florida

Deshaun Watson

In the 2015 season, Deshaun Watson set records for most total yards in championship game history. He was the first player ever to pass more than 4,000 yards in one season. He was also a **Heisman Memorial Trophy** candidate two years running. Watson led the Tigers to their 2017 National Championship win, completing 36 of 56 passes for three touchdowns against Alabama's top-ranked defense. He also threw a last-second, game-winning pass to Hunter Renfrow. He was awarded the Offensive **Most Valuable Player (MVP)** Award for the game. In 2017, Watson was **drafted** 12th overall in the NFL draft by the Houston Texans, where he still plays today.

Position: Quarterback
Seasons: 2014–2016 (Clemson Tigers), 2017–Present (Houston Texans)
Born: September 14, 1995, Gainesville, Georgia

Terry Kinard

Terry Kinard began his college career with difficulty. He was injured in his first game and out the rest of the season. He was grateful for the chance to redshirt. Redshirting is when a player skips his freshman season in order to gain an extra year as an eligible NCAA player. The next year, he came back stronger. Kinard was a two-time first-team All-American while playing for the Tigers. He was named CBS National Defensive Player of the Year in 1982. He holds Clemson's all-time records for interceptions and for tackles by a defensive back. The New York Giants drafted Kinard 10th overall in 1983. Kinard retired from the NFL in 1990 and was inducted into the College Football Hall of Fame in 2001.

Position: Defensive Back
Seasons: 1978–1982 (Clemson Tigers), 1983–1989 (New York Giants), 1990 (Houston Oilers)
Born: November 24, 1959, Bitburg, West Germany

DeAndre Hopkins

DeAndre Hopkins, nicknamed "Nuk," was Clemson's leading receiver as a true freshman, with 52 receptions. In his junior year, he scored a school-record 18 touchdowns. Hopkins decided to skip his senior season to enter the NFL draft. Despite a calf injury, he was ranked as a top-five wide receiver **prospect**. The Houston Texans picked him in the first round of the 2013 draft. He started during his second year in the NFL. In 2017, he led the league with scoring among wide receivers and was named first team **All-Pro**. Hopkins remains a vital part of the Texans' offense.

Position: Wide Receiver
Seasons: 2010–2012 (Clemson Tigers), 2013–Present (Houston Texans)
Born: June 6, 1992, Central, South Carolina

All-Time Records

11,904

Career Passing Yards

Tajh Boyd passed for 11,904 yards over his career from 2010 to 2013.

0.914

Winning Percentage

Deshaun Watson has the top winning percentage of any quarterback, 0.914 over three years. He had a 32–3 record from 2014 to 2016.

186

Tackles

Keith Adams completed the most tackles in a single year in 1999, with 186 during his sophomore year.

1,658

Passing Yards

Travis Etienne set Clemson's single-season record for passing yards in 2018, with 1,658. He also broke the single-season touchdown record in 2018, with 24.

7,718

Team Passing Yards

In 2015, Clemson passed for 7,718 yards, led by Deshaun Watson. They nearly broke this record again in 2016 with 7,555 yards.

Timeline

Throughout the team's history, the Clemson Tigers have had many memorable events that have become defining moments for the team and its fans.

In 1896, Clemson football plays its inaugural football season.

1900
The team has its first undefeated year.

1942
On September 19, Memorial Stadium opens.

1953
On May 8, Clemson joins the Atlantic Coast Conference.

1954
On September 18, head cheerleader George Bennett fires a cannon after each Tigers score, a tradition that continues today.

1956
The team defeats Virginia 7–0 at Clemson to clinch the Tigers' first-ever ACC Championship.

1966
On September 24, the Tigers run past Howard's Rock for the first time and then defeat Virginia, beginning a tradition that continues to this day.

1900 1920 1940 1960

1982
On January 1, Clemson wins its first National Championship over Nebraska in the 48th **annual** Orange Bowl Classic. This win completes its first undefeated season since 1948. It is the university's first National Championship in any sport.

1983
A record 10 Clemson players are chosen in the NFL draft. They are led by Terry Kinard, who is chosen 10th overall by the New York Giants.

On November 12, 1988, Clemson wins an ACC record-tying third-straight ACC title at Maryland.

1983
The north upper deck of Memorial Stadium is used for the first time on September 3 in a victory over Western Carolina, bringing the seating capacity to more than 80,000.

1980

2000

2020

The Future
Clemson has stronger coaching and recruiting than ever. They also have new facilities, including a new complex nicknamed "Dabo's World" after Coach Swinney. Dabo's World includes lounges, locker rooms, training facilities, and coaches' offices. The Tigers are not only continuing the team's historical greatness, but also improving upon it. They are eager to win more championships in the future.

2018
The 2018 season is one of the most successful in Tigers football history. The Tigers end with a 15–0 record. They win a fourth consecutive ACC title, the Cotton Bowl, and the National Championship.

Write a Biography

Life Story

A person's life story can be the subject of a book. This kind of book is called a biography. Biographies often describe the lives of people who have achieved great success. These people may be alive today, or they may have lived many years ago. Reading a biography can help you learn more about a great person.

Get the Facts

Use this book, and research in the library and on the internet, to find out more about your favorite player. Learn as much about him as you can. What position does he play? What are his statistics in important categories? Has he set any records? Also, be sure to write down key events in the person's life. What was his childhood like? What has he accomplished off the field? Is there anything else that makes this person special or unusual?

Use the Concept Web

A concept web is a useful research tool. Read the questions in the concept web on the following page. Answer the questions in your notebook. Your answers will help you write a biography.

Concept Web

Adulthood
- Where does this individual currently reside?
- Does he have a family?

Your Opinion
- What did you learn from the books you read in your research?
- Would you suggest these books to others?
- Was anything missing from these books?

Childhood
- Where and when was this person born?
- Describe his parents, siblings, and friends.
- Did this person grow up in unusual circumstances?

Accomplishments off the Field
- What is this person's life's work?
- Has he received awards or recognition for accomplishments?
- How have this person's accomplishments served others?

Write a Biography

Help and Obstacles
- Did this individual have a positive attitude?
- Did he receive help from others?
- Did this person have a mentor?
- Did this person face any hardships?
- If so, how were the hardships overcome?

Accomplishments on the Field
- What records does this person hold?
- What key games and plays have defined his career?
- What are his stats in categories important to his position?

Work and Preparation
- What was this person's education?
- What was his work experience?
- How does this person work?
- What is the process he uses?

Trivia Time

Take this quiz to test your knowledge of the Clemson Tigers. The answers are printed upside down under each question.

1 How many times have the Tigers been National Champions, and in what years?

A. Three times, in 1981, 2016, and 2018

2 What are Clemson University's official colors?

A. Burnt orange and purple

3 Which former Clemson player was the first Tiger in the Pro Football Hall of Fame?

A. Brian Dawkins

4 What is the name of the team's newest mascot?

A. Tiger Cub

5 What head coach has the most wins ever for Clemson?

A. Frank Howard

6 What quarterback holds the record for highest winning percentage?

A. Deshaun Watson

7 What is the team logo of the Clemson Tigers?

A. A tiger paw

8 What is the nickname of Memorial Stadium?

A. Death Valley

9 What conference do the Tigers belong to?

A. Atlantic Coast Conference

10 Who is Clemson's biggest rival?

A. University of South Carolina

Key Words

All-Pro: a term used to designate the best players of each position during a given season

annual: something that occurs once a year

drafted: chosen to play professionally in the National Football League during an annual event

Hall of Fame: a group of persons judged to be outstanding in a particular sport

Heisman Memorial Trophy: an annual award given to the college football player who best demonstrates excellence and hard work

innovations: new ideas or methods

logo: a symbol that stands for a team or organization

Most Valuable Player (MVP): the player judged to be most valuable to his team's success

National Champions: top achievers for any sport or contest in a particular nation

postseason: a sporting event that takes place after the end of the regular season

prospect: a player who is likely to succeed in a sport at a high level

recruiting: working to enroll someone as a member of an organization

Index

Log on to www.av2books.com

AV² by Weigl brings you media enhanced books that support active learning. Go to www.av2books.com, and enter the special code found on page 2 of this book. You will gain access to enriched and enhanced content that supplements and complements this book. Content includes video, audio, weblinks, quizzes, a slideshow, and activities.

AV² Online Navigation

Audio
Listen to sections of the book read aloud.

Book Pages
AV² pages directly correspond to pages in the book.

Video
Watch informative video clips.

Embedded Weblinks
Gain additional information for research.

Key Words
Study vocabulary, and complete a matching word activity.

Try This!
Complete activities and hands-on experiments.

Quizzes
Test your knowledge.

Slideshow
View images and captions, and prepare a presentation.

AV² was built to bridge the gap between print and digital. We encourage you to tell us what you like and what you want to see in the future.

Sign up to be an AV² Ambassador at www.av2books.com/ambassador.

Due to the dynamic nature of the internet, some of the URLs and activities provided as part of AV² by Weigl may have changed or ceased to exist. AV² by Weigl accepts no responsibility for any such changes. All media enhanced books are regularly monitored to update addresses and sites in a timely manner. Contact AV² by Weigl at 1-866-649-3445 or av2books@weigl.com with any questions, comments, or feedback.